where two
or three...

Other relevant titles

Children and Bereavement
2nd edition

Wendy Duffy

Connecting with RE
RE and faith development for children with autism and/or severe and complex learning disabilities

Liz O'Brien

Not Just Sunday
Setting up and running mid-week clubs for children

Margaret Withers

Special Children, Special Needs
Integrating children with disabilities and special needs into your church

Simon Bass

help and advice for churches
with few or no children

where two or three...

Margaret Withers

CHURCH HOUSE
PUBLISHING

Church House Publishing

Church House

Great Smith Street

London SW1P 3NZ

ISBN 0 7151 4028 0

Published 2004 by Church House Publishing

Printed in England by Halstan & Co. Ltd,
Amersham, Bucks

Contents

Acknowledgements

The author wishes to thank the Revd Colette Thornborough, vicar of St Nicholas, Blundellsands, Liverpool, for giving her time and help to tell her about the creation of the toddler group, JUICE, and her permission for it to be recorded in this book.

The other stories and examples are events that have happened during the last eight years, but as both the churches and the children will have moved on since they were recorded, they have been given imaginary names to protect their identities.

1 Introduction

You have opened this book because you care about children. You want them to hear the Christian story. You want to see them filling your church, but, somehow, it does not seem to be happening.

Maybe you have just two or three children at church on Sunday, or maybe you have none at all. Dozens of youngsters may pass your door every day or you may live in a rural or inner city community where there are very few children.

This book has been written to help you to find a way of having a ministry among the local children, even if you have nothing or very little at present. You may be a vicar, minister or member of a church council who recognizes the need to develop or re-establish a ministry among children, or you may be the leader of a tiny group of youngsters. Whatever your situation, this book will give you ideas for developing the children's work that you already have, or ways in which you can start from the beginning. There are suggestions for engaging with children in the community, working with other churches, and drawing children together from small villages and hamlets.

Each chapter is free-standing. You may want to read them through in order but, if you have no children's work or children at your church at all, you may want to start with Chapter 2, 'Precious few!', and then move on to Chapter 6, 'No children in church', and Chapter 7, 'Communities with few children', before reading the material about particular situations.

The vast majority of churches ground their work and worship on Sunday. This has been the pattern for two thousand years, but changes in working patterns and lifestyle have eroded the traditional pattern of the week. Churches need to engage with people where they are and this is especially so with children and young people. Whatever your situation, see that you read Chapter 8, 'Seven whole days', and Chapter 9, 'United we stand' as well as the 'golden rules' in Appendix A. A holistic approach is vital if your children's ministry is going to develop. Stories and examples have been included throughout the text.

You may feel that you want to blame someone for the lack of children in your church. If you are a children's worker you may feel very isolated and even angry. If you live in an area where there are very few children anyway you may have a sense of bereavement, especially if you have seen the community dwindle and amenities reduced over the years. You are not alone! Other churches are in the same position. As you read this book, you will gain ideas for working with tiny numbers and scant resources. You may even find that you have contact with more children than you had thought.

Jesus said:

'Are not two sparrows sold for a penny? Yet not one of them will fall to the ground unperceived by your Father. And even the hairs of your head are all counted. So do not be afraid; you are of more value than many sparrows.'

Matthew 10.29-31

2 Precious few!

Start where you are

Think about the children that you have at your church.

- Do you have a few coming on Sunday but feel unsure about how to welcome and involve them?

- Are you leading a tiny group of children of mixed ages?

- Do you see children passing the church and wish that somehow they would come through the door?

- Or do you have no children at all?

Take care of your valuables

Children are one of the Church's most valuable assets. They are also the most vulnerable, so your ministry with them is a vitally important one. There are no magic answers or quick-fix solutions for your church if it has only a few or no children, but in nearly every situation, there are ways of engaging with youngsters in the locality and giving them opportunities to hear the gospel message.

Churches with a few children have two special qualities: their children are precious individuals, and the children's work is inevitably fragile. As with any other precious and delicate gifts, they need extra special care. Jesus described children as signs of the kingdom. Behind every child is an image of God.

If your children are genuinely part of the church family and their ministry is accepted, that is a great blessing. If you have a little group that is well run, with imaginatively prepared sessions and the children enjoy the occasional celebration, they will grow in faith and love of God. Whatever the pressures, they will be inclined to stay with their faith as they grow up.

Create an environment

Let us start our journey of discovery by looking at the positive side of your situation.

You are probably thinking that, if more children came to your church, everything would be all right. That is not necessarily true in the short term. How would you cope if twenty new children suddenly arrived at your church next Sunday? It takes skill, people and resources to welcome and provide worship and nurture for a large number of children, especially at short notice, but do not panic! We can all create an environment in which we are prepared for the unexpected and ready for growth should it happen.

Think positively

So, before we go further with our reflection and planning, let's count our blessings by making the best of what we have – a very small number of children. Then, not only will they flourish but, if a new family happens to come to your church, there will be a little bunch of children that is happy and ready to welcome them and make them want to come again.

Small is beautiful

There are positive benefits in having a small group of children. Indeed, some parents make considerable sacrifices to send children to a school where they will be taught in a small class. There can be the same benefits for the small number of children at church. Every child can be well known and valued as an individual. Every adult in the congregation can learn and address each child by name. Every child can contribute to the worship and be able to talk about things that interest him or her and to ask questions. Ways of doing this with a mixed-age group are discussed in Chapter 5, 'Challenges and issues'.

Meeting places

There are far more meeting places for a small group than a large one. It can meet in a room, even in someone's house, which may be more comfortable and pleasant than a hall. If you are meeting in the church or hall, there are many ways in which it can be made attractive with a little planning. This is discussed in detail in Chapter 4, 'The children's own session'.

Celebrations

Celebrate everything that you do. Display pictures, sing 'Happy Birthday', give out Easter eggs and Christingles, even if you only have two children. Make the children feel valued as, indeed, God values each one of them.

If you decide to have an outing, it is possible to travel on public transport or in a couple of cars. It is easier to take a small group to a theatre, or visitor attraction, or to a local or diocesan festival where space or bookings are limited. Outings and events can be organized at short notice when only a couple of families are involved.

The next step

It is not easy to have a ministry with two or three children or to sustain enthusiasm when building the first links with a new generation, but with a will to succeed, much can be done. You have taken the first steps towards this by starting to read this book!

Most of children's ministry takes place on Sunday so let us move forward on our journey by focusing on the worship and nurture that takes place then.

3 Sunday morning in church

Rejoice!

If there are any children at your church, the chances are that they will meet on Sunday during the morning service. They may be the children of one or two families, or they may be youngsters who are staying with their grandparents. There may occasionally be unaccompanied children who have enjoyed a special service and decided to return. Whatever the reason, having children in church is a blessing and a cause for rejoicing.

Welcoming children

Why do we feel the need to welcome children to church? That may seem a stupid question. Your answers will include that they must be made to feel part of the worshipping congregation, that, if they are not catered for, they will go away, and that is true.

Think a little further. Why do we need to welcome children into a church that already belongs to them? Children are agents of God's mission in the world: 'Whoever welcomes this child in my name welcomes me, and whoever welcomes me welcomes the one who sent me' (Luke 9.48).

Children are members of the Church, God's family, through baptism. At a local level, each child is part of the 'cure of souls' of the parish and may be the offspring of active members of the congregation. Your church is their church. Whatever we do, a change of thinking will be needed to underpin it. Then it will not be about welcoming children, (them) into (our) church, but about us all being welcome as equal and valued members of a family.

How do we carry this out in practice when welcoming children as part of the worshipping family?

1. Do we welcome everyone by greeting people in the porch or by leaving the door standing open?

2. Do we greet the children by name?

3. Do we take an active interest in them: 'Did you have a nice holiday?', 'Is your cold better?', or do we reserve these pleasantries for adults?

4. If we have printed service sheets, do we offer a large-print one to young readers as well as elderly people, or have one with pictures that can be coloured in?

5. Do we help a visitor with young children by offering to sit with them, showing where toilets are and generally being supportive?

6. Do we offer children's service books, or *Communion* or *Lord's Prayer Cubes*?

7. Do we have toys and books available should a child get restless?

8. Do we make it clear by our behaviour that a toddler taking a dash up the aisle or a baby crying is part of being a child and we are not put off by it?

If the answer to any of these questions is 'no', take steps to rectify it immediately. Suggestions 1–5 are basic courtesies and cost nothing. Suggestions 6–7 are about being prepared for any children that come to the church. You will know the best level of provision according to your resources, but, if you have books and toys, they should be clean and in good condition. The last suggestion is about affirming children as they are, rather than expecting them to behave as adults, which they are not.

As we have already discussed, we are presented with opportunities but also challenges for providing worship and nurture that is appropriate for all ages and stages of faith.

Together or apart

Do you have worship for all ages together or should you have a separate session for the children? This is not just a case of having leaders or teachers, but also depends largely on the facilities. Ask yourself where the children would be happier and able to enjoy various activities. If the church is cold and there is a pleasant room or hall, or even a room in the vicarage, go there. If the option is a dark and dreary vestry where the session has to be conducted in a whisper and halt every time the organ plays, perhaps they would be better off in church.

Forget the mistaken assumptions that the right place for the children is to be apart or that the service belongs to the adults. Ask what is the best provision for the children in your particular situation. Then work towards making it happen. That may be about place and style of nurture but it will also include questions about the style of worship and the role that children play in it.

Children in church

The most common assumption about children in church is that the services are unsuitable for them, and unless they can behave and worship like adults, they should be kept out of sight and certainly out of hearing. That is a complete denial of Jesus' teaching. He set the child in the centre and was scathing with the disciples that tried to keep them away from him.

If you decide to have your children in church throughout the service, this needs to be treated positively. Ideally, it will be because you have realized the value of families and the Church family worshipping together, but you may not be ready for that step yet. On a practical level, it may be because the numbers of children are too small and erratic or because there is nowhere else for them to go. Whatever the reason, having made the decision for them to be in church, they must be welcomed and involved as equal and valuable members of the Christian family.

Children with parents

As ongoing support to the parents who have their children sitting with them, encourage them to bring quiet toys and suggest that the children wear slippers if they are inclined to run about. Provide children's service books, and *Lord's Prayer* and *Communion Cubes*, a simple and popular form of the Rubik's cube.

Have a few cloth bags containing a picture book, soft toy, etc. for the youngest children and folders containing a storybook with a worksheet for the older children. These must be regularly cleaned and replenished.

See that the clergy or worship leaders are aware of the mixed ages and are inclusive in speaking and teaching. This includes briefing any visiting preachers. Most clergy cope well with the occasional child taking a dash up the aisle or offering a teddy bear but they cope better if they are prepared.

See that the children are given service sheets or hymn books whether they can read or not, and see that at least one hymn is easy to sing with maybe a chorus so that the children can join in without difficulty.

During the service

If a child is familiar with church, he or she may be happy to join in the responses, look at a children's service book, sing the hymns – even with the hymn book upside down – and say, 'amen' on every occasion. With practice and a welcoming atmosphere, children soon learn what is expected of them. There will be times when it seems to a child that nothing is happening, and he or she will need things to look at or to do. This is not necessarily a time to opt out, but to make the most of the surroundings and action. Worship that uses colour and movement as well as sound has a lot to offer a child.

Involving children actively in the worship

Leading worship is a team activity and most of the roles can be taken by children as well as adults. Children's ministries in worship, their reverence and concentration can teach adults a great deal. If they are involved in various tasks, being put on a rota with adults will do much to affirm their position as equal members of the congregation.

Many children read well. They are used to reading aloud in school so can read in church. Children have less cluttered perceptions about the needs of the world and their neighbours. They can lead intercessions that are short and to the point. Many children enjoy serving and some enjoy singing or playing a musical instrument.

Most children, except the very shy or nervous ones, can welcome the people as they arrive and give out service sheets. Every child can put the numbers on the hymn board, help to take the collection, and present the gifts at the Offertory.

The children's session in church

In the Eucharist, the inactive time (for a child) is between the Collect and the Offertory. The readings are followed by a sermon, then the Creed and then the Intercessions. That will take up to half an hour, nearly as long as the rest of the service put together. If the service is not a Eucharist, the times when just one person is speaking are more broken up but there will still be readings, a sermon and prayers.

You may wish to use this time for teaching the children. Have a low table and chairs set up in a corner or near to the back of the church where the children can meet. If there is an area such as a vestry or enclosed porch, have it prepared for the session. A great deal can be done in twenty minutes if it is properly prepared. If you are able to read a Bible story, use a large illustrated copy so that the children can see the pictures. If you can only speak quietly, encourage the children to sit near you and make the most of the pictures or visual aids rather than speaking all of the time. There are a variety of suitable pop-up books of Bible stories. Have modelling clay or play dough and other craft materials as well as the usual colouring books or sheets. Provide other books suitable for all ages for the children who would rather read quietly.

This kind of area could be used formally as described above or as an area that a child can withdraw to if he or she has become restless in the pew.

Bring the children back to their families in time for the Peace or the next hymn and encourage them to stay there or sit with you for the rest of the service.

Children and Holy Communion

If your children are worshipping at the Eucharist frequently, consider whether it would be appropriate to admit them to Holy Communion before Confirmation. The question here concerns when one or two children are worshipping at the Eucharist each Sunday and asks whether the fellowship should be completed by their receiving Holy Communion alongside the other worshippers.

The majority of Anglican dioceses, the Methodist and the United Reformed Churches admit children, but it is advisable to check your diocesan or denominational policy before entering into discussion.

The many theological, historical and pastoral issues surrounding this subject are beyond the scope of this book and every situation is different. What is clear, however, is that the situation and decisions facing a church with two children who worship at the Eucharist with forty adults each week, are very different from those of the church with twenty children who have their own session and are only present at part of the service or attend it infrequently. If you want to explore this further, ask your diocesan children's adviser to help you to explore the whole process as a congregation.

A story of welcome: Including Anthony

The church at Fakeham St Lawrence stood at the end of the village street. Every Sunday, a small group of young children met in the rectory for a Bible story and some activities. Then they trekked up the footpath to the church to show the congregation what they had been doing, join in the final prayers and hymn and then meet their parents.

Every child, that is, except Anthony. Anthony was nine. He had a lovely treble voice and enjoyed singing in the choir with his parents and a dozen other adults. In fact, Anthony was a valued member of the choir and congregation in every way but one. Everyone at the service except Anthony received Holy Communion.

An open meeting was held to discuss whether the children should be allowed to receive Holy Communion. It was soon realized that the discussion was principally about Anthony. Anthony was asked if he would like to say anything. He got slowly to his feet and said simply, 'Well, I do feel left out.' The assembled people agreed that this should not be so. Anthony was admitted to the fellowship of Holy Communion on Easter Day. This affirmed his place as part of the gathered community and paved the way for the younger children to become more involved in the worship when the time was right.

---

4 The children's own session

High standards

If you decide that it will be best for the children if they have a separate worship and nurture session on a Sunday morning, you will need certain minimum resources:

- appropriate standards of safety and childcare;
- at least two adults to lead each session;
- a pleasant and suitable venue;
- the ongoing support of the church council and congregation.

However small the numbers, each child is important and deserves the best that you can provide.

Safety and child protection

There is a tendency to lower standards with a small group, using the excuse that they are not necessary when there are only a few children. They are just as important and should be easier to maintain with small numbers. See that you always have two adults to lead your children's group and that they have been through the Criminal Records Bureau enhanced check and accepted by the church council.

Check that the place where you hold the children's session is safe with no trailing flex or cords, piles of chairs or areas where young children can climb. If you are in a small room, see that there is space to move safely, with as little clutter as possible. Invest in a couple of plastic crates, one for the resources for the worship, the other for materials for craft or other activities, so that you can keep the space tidy.

If you have a walk to or from church, see that you have enough adults, especially with very young children, to escort them and help with crossing roads.

Venues

Insist that the children meet in a place that is pleasant and conducive to learning and worship. A cold and dirty vestry or a corner where the session is conducted in whispers is unsuitable, however few children are in it.

As discussed in Chapter 2, 'Precious few!', one of the advantages of a small group is that it can meet in a room or somebody's house, which is often more pleasant than a church hall. Some churches have a narthex or an area under the church tower, which makes a small place to meet. A church which no longer needs a separate choir vestry could turn that into a pleasant meeting room with a little ingenuity.

Setting up a children's corner in the church itself is becoming popular again, with low tables and chairs and some books and toys. A children's corner may become the children's own chapel with a small altar. Creating a children's area in church would be a good way to introduce youngsters who are not familiar with church to the building, and the area could be used on Sundays if you decide to hold the children's own session in church as suggested in the previous chapter.

If you meet in a church hall, use the space imaginatively. It can seem very large and unfriendly to a small group of children. Set up an area for worship and story telling. If you are having a craft session, prepare a table in another area, and keep a large space for games and another one for refreshments.

Preparation

Prepare the room or hall beforehand so that the children know that you are ready for them. If you have an area for worship or if you are meeting around a table, set it with a cross, Bible and maybe flowers and candles. Consider having a visual aid to set the scene and be a talking point. Take as much trouble to prepare a session for three children as for thirty, and be prepared to be flexible.

If you have escorted the children from church, see that they arrive at the hall or room in an orderly manner. It is fine to chat happily on the way but racing ahead and arriving out of breath and overexcited is not conducive to worship or learning. Stand by the door and ask quietly if everyone is ready to go in to sit in the worship area or around the table. Remind the children to hang up coats and wipe their shoes if that is necessary. Speak slowly and deliberately.

If the children are being dropped off by their parents, welcome them at the door and see that they have something to play with or read until the session starts. Have some music playing to set the atmosphere. Be ready to welcome a newcomer or someone who attends occasionally.

Outline of the session

There is no such thing as a typical session because every group of youngsters is different and so will be their relationships with each other and with the rest of the congregation. A possible framework could be something like this:

Sit quietly with the children and turn the music off gradually to create a feeling of silence and expectancy. If the children have come straight from home, start by greeting them by their names and introducing the theme of the day. Show that the worship is about to begin by lighting a candle, or having a special group song or prayer. Follow this with a short time to think about the things that have gone wrong since you last met, the times that we have been unkind to other people or let ourselves down. Say sorry to God and be thankful that he gives us a chance to start again.

If you have been in the first part of the main service, it will probably be enough to introduce the theme for the day by recalling together what you have just heard and seen. Make a link with that worship by lighting a candle or saying your group prayer. It is a good idea to take the collection at an early point to prevent coins rolling over the floor.

Detailed information on organizing worship and involving each child is given later in this chapter.

Depending on the ages and backgrounds of the children, you may want to start by drawing out ideas about the theme or look at the visual aid and use it as a starting point. Read the Bible story from an edition with illustrations or have a time of sharing the information if the children already know it. If you enjoy telling stories, use your own words and engage with the children through your tone of voice, timing and body language. This will be the best way with a very mixed-age group if you can do it well.

Follow the story with an activity that the children can do together or, if they are an older group, have an open discussion. Examples of activities for mixed-age groups and suitable programmes will be found in Chapter 5, 'Challenges and issues'.

If the group is going into church, organize who will take in the collection bag or any work to be displayed. Finish by giving out any notices and then moving calmly into church. If the session ends with the children being collected, end with a prayer time, any news, birthday celebrations and even a song.

Stay smiling

When two children are absent from school, it is scarcely noticed. If two children are missing from a church group, it can halve the numbers and skew the level of teaching and activities. Never let the children feel that you are annoyed or cannot do something because of lack of numbers, however frustrated you may feel. As we have already discussed, there are advantages of having a small group and each child is precious.

Managing a small group

Be clear about your aims and boundaries and stick to them. This may seem very defensive but small groups are often put under pressure. It may be that your group is seen to be unimportant because of its size or that it is assumed that the leader will have plenty of energy to deal with other things at the same time as teaching and leading worship with children.

Make it clear that your session is the children's worship time, the nurture group or whatever club you are leading. Guard against your group being a crèche as well. While welcoming a parent who joins you with a restless youngster, never attempt to look after unaccompanied babies or toddlers while nurturing other children.

If you are meeting in the church hall, see that your time with the children is respected and not interrupted by adults moving furniture, talking or clattering crockery.

You will probably not have discipline problems if you know your children well, but should a child be having a bad day or be upset, arrange for one adult to work with that child while the others do a different activity. Do not let this be thought of as a punishment, but a way of giving time and attention where it is needed.

Worship

Let every child take an active role in the worship: lighting a candle to remind everyone that Jesus is the light of the world, taking the collection in a small bag or bowl, reading the story or saying a special group prayer.

Talk together about the visual aid. If it is a single item, invite the children to handle it, smell it or taste it, and so on. Lead gently from this into the theme for the day or the Bible story. Use a large and attractive edition of the Bible so that the children can see and share the pictures.

Lead the prayers by asking the children what they want to thank God for, and then what they want to tell him about, so that every child can offer petitions. Always say the Lord's Prayer and have a special prayer for the group. Include praying for the adults in the church building, the children who are not there and children at other churches. This would help the children to remember that, although they are few in number, they are part of a big family, the Church.

Music

Music is a vital part of any worship. Recorded music can do much to set the atmosphere before worship or when the children move to and from the church building. Instrumental music can also be effective and used to teach and accompany songs and hymns. Singing can be tricky with a small group but it is worth trying if an adult is confident enough to lead it. Young children will usually try to join in. Singing unaccompanied is often the most effective way of learning songs and hymns with small groups.

If you need to choose some music, find out what hymns or songs are used at your local school. That will ensure that the music is suitable for young children and that a few of them will know it already. Short repetitive songs with choruses, rounds and canons (even though you will not have enough children to sing in two parts) are effective with small groups. Lively, rhythmic songs are best saved for large groups with a strong accompaniment.

Joining the rest of the congregation

Whether the children meet in church for the opening part of the service or are dropped off at the room or hall ten minutes before it starts will depend on its location. The most effective way is for the children to start in church and then leave for their own session, but, if the room or hall is some distance from the church, this is impractical, especially in poor weather, and a waste of time. Use your own judgement, but see that, if a child appears at church but would like to join the session, there is someone to welcome and escort him or her to the hall or room.

It is important, however, that the children and adults worship together for some part of the service. When the children join the rest of the congregation in church, let them sit with their parents or together at the front where they can see clearly. One child could take up the collection with the rest of the Offertory. If they have done any art or craft, it could be presented at the same time. This has the twofold effect of linking the children's nurture and worship into the main service, and reminding us that the children's gifts, however small, are precious in the eyes of God.

Occasional groups

If a weekly group is too difficult or small to sustain, have a Family Service or an all-age Eucharist once a month and hold the Junior Church once a month. Publicize it clearly on the church notice board and in the parish magazine or news-sheet. Flexible working, divided families and relations living a distance from home put a great deal of pressure on Sunday, but some families will organize their lives so that they can attend the Family Service or on the Sunday when there is a Junior Church for their children.

Supporting children's leaders

We have discussed how important it is to see that the children are valued as individuals and that their activities are given as much thought and consideration as they would be if there were a large group. The same applies to the children's leaders. They have a valuable ministry and an enormous responsibility. As well as ensuring that the leader always has a second adult to provide support by helping with the session and dealing with any problem that may occur, have a reserve who can take the children if the usual leader is ill or on holiday. This may be difficult if you have a tiny congregation, but a parent of one of the children or an elderly former leader may help occasionally. It is putting an unfair burden on a committed leader to cancel the children's session because of one person's absence.

Provide a budget for children's work, however small, and encourage your leader to go on training days. A small group is fragile so needs a capable and confident leader. Moreover, the children's leader will find that she or he is surrounded with other people who have small groups and similar issues and needs. People working with children in the Church often have low self-worth and need this sort of encouragement.

See that the children's group is prayed for regularly in church and that the children's leaders are thanked formally at the Annual General Meeting.

5 Challenges and issues

Challenges to be overcome

Having discovered that we can view our ministry with a small number of children positively, let us turn to the difficulties and see how they can be seen as challenges that can be overcome with ingenuity and thought.

Mixed ages

The principal difficulty of having a small group of children is if they are of very mixed ages. It will stretch your ingenuity to provide significant worship and nurture that is accessible to the youngest children while challenging the eldest.

You will soon find out what each child enjoys doing and what his or her strengths and weaknesses are. Give each child a role in the worship according to their age and capabilities. The oldest can light the candle before the worship, and the youngest can blow it out at the end. Youngsters who have an aptitude can read the Bible story or play a musical instrument. Anyone can take the collection, organize recorded music or start the group prayer. Everyone can say 'amen' at the end.

See that you give plenty of opportunities to the fluent reader or quick thinker so that he or she is still mentally stretched. Be prepared to listen and engage with him or her. The throwaway question is often the one that the youngster really wants to ask. For the youngest child or one with learning difficulties, offer larger print, simpler versions or opportunities to draw instead of write if that is more appropriate.

Be cautious with programmes that depend on a high level of literacy or have highly competitive activities. It is glaringly obvious when one child out of three or four has difficulty reading or always comes last.

Some activities are suitable for a small mixed-age group and are popular with children of all ages. They include making a collage or a banner, cooking, puppets, candle making, brass rubbing and finding things in the churchyard or church building.

The oldest children

One of the challenges of any mixed-age group is to give the oldest children activities that respect their age and dignity. It is not just a case of keeping them occupied or letting them help. With a small group where one child is older than all the others, whether it is an eight-year-old girl with three toddlers, or an eleven-year-old boy with youngsters of six and seven, the challenge is to stretch and challenge them and give them a sense of self-worth. It is not good for a growing youngster's credibility with his peers to be seen to be with 'the babies'. Always see that he or she is learning as well as helping, and try to give time for conversation and engagement.

It is encouraging if the eldest child turns up happily and is content to be with younger children but keep your eyes open for the first signs of disaffection. In the short term, it may be fine for an older child to play with the babies or read quietly, but children change rapidly, and a few signs of restlessness will soon lead to opting out.

Using gifts and interests

Find your eldest children's strengths and interests and encourage them. If they are good at craft, offer, for example, some materials for making a puppet out of a sock with felt and glitter decorations, while the other children are making puppets with paper plates and crayons. If a youngster enjoys reading aloud, let her tell the story or act it out in dialogue with you. If he plays a musical instrument, let him contribute to the worship.

Never insist that a youngster takes part in activities like acting out or singing action songs. Some older children enjoy them, but others do not.

Leadership

If the youngster relates well to the other children, ask him or her to take a leadership role. This could include asking the children to line up, sitting with the youngest child in church, helping with finding places in books and supervising clearing up. If children are being used as assistants in this way, treat them as such by involving them in planning meetings, and asking them for their opinions or suggestions. Remember to praise excellence when they have done something special rather than dismissing it because the child is older than his companions.

Enquiring and searching

One of the trickiest situations is teaching the truths about God to a group with different levels of understanding and perceptions. This is so for any congregation, and even more challenging when the older child wants to explore and question, usually in the middle of a story or discussion.

If the child is not at ease with listening to children's Bible stories, consider offering the *Bible for Children*, which is based on the New Jerusalem Bible. It consists of modified extracts from the text with references for the sections that have been omitted. There are background information and marginal notes as well as fantasy-style illustrations, and it would be suitable for any keen reader of over ten years.

Remember that the stories in the Bible were written as a way of trying to explain things that we do not understand, the nature and ways of God. Perhaps answering with another question such as 'What do you think?' or 'What does it mean to you?' and listening to the answer can satisfy the questioner without interrupting the flow of the story. It can be picked up later, maybe when the other adult is helping clear up or doing another activity.

Never brush aside a child's sceptical comment or make him or her feel that it is wrong to have honest queries or doubts. Be prepared to admit your own doubts and lack of knowledge. After all, faith is a lifelong journey and we are all on it together!

Programmes

Unfortunately, there are very few resources to support a ministry with a small group of children of mixed ages. Most Sunday and holiday club programmes are designed for large and well-resourced groups and the various activities are not always adaptable for a small group of children with few facilities.

Your diocesan children's adviser will probably have a collection of resources that you can borrow to find which suits your group best.

If you decide to use a teaching programme, look through it carefully and avoid sessions with activities that require large numbers. They are quite easy to spot because, for example, they involve dividing the children into teams or have drama that needs several actors.

An added caution is that some of the large glossy programmes that offer separate teaching for children of different ages are designed for three separate groups rather than three individuals. It can be demoralizing to spend a large sum of money on a wonderful course but then find that only a small part of it can be used as it stands.

Suitable programmes

Some teaching materials can be used with a small group:

The worship and nurture programme *Roots* is flexible in content and can be adapted for children of different ages and for use in all-age worship. Readers can also subscribe to a web site that offers up to date and accessible material.

Although a bigger financial layout is needed, *Godly Play*, a method of learning based on Montessori teaching, is highly suitable for using with small groups of any age from toddlers to adults. It seeks to develop natural interests and activities by allowing children to explore a Bible story in their own way and think through their own questions and suppositions in a calm atmosphere.

CURBS (Children in URBan Situations) produces accessible resources that are suitable for children of different ages and levels of understanding.

Rural Sunrise is a non-denominational organization that specializes in work with rural and other small churches. It provides biblically based resources and training.

The Scripture Union programme *Light*, which replaces *Salt*, has activities that are designed for small groups but can be adapted for larger ones.

Details of these organizations and programmes are listed in Appendix B.

Moving on

However you organize your sessions, encourage the oldest children to become part of the main congregation on some Sundays by being servers, giving out the books, operating the sound system, reading or leading the intercessions. Eventually, they will be there every week. It is called growing up.

A story of vision: JUICE

The parish of St Nicholas, Blundellsands, in the Anglican Diocese of Liverpool, recognized that it had several needs but was not sure how to move forward. The new vicar, Colette, organized a PCC day to discuss the vision for the parish. It identified four areas, one being children and youth, and from this sprung the idea of a toddler group. The church had a spacious hall, and there were always young families in the vicinity so the plant and potential were there, but what should they call it? Names were invented and rejected, but then Faye, a teenage helper with the Brownie pack, had a brainwave: 'Call it "Juice" – Join us in Christ's environment.'

The next step was to find a leader. Several people were willing to help but, after anxious praying and searching, Sue, a former nursery manager, came forward. A few others, including a couple of retired people, offered to provide a welcome and refreshments, and all was in place to open on 8 October 2003, nearly a year after the original meeting.

Fears that nobody would turn up proved groundless. News of the club was spread through baptismal families and word of mouth. After three weeks, there were twenty-five children and a waiting list. Just six months later, there were up to forty youngsters and JUICE was considering operating a parallel group on a second day.

What made JUICE so successful? Colette believes that the time for prayer and careful planning was vital; so was having an orderly programme, with the hall set out with space for craft, toys and a baby-playing area with circle time at the end for everyone. The local Press has also proved a great ally. Parents have spoken of the low charges: JUICE is non-profit-making and any extra money is ploughed back into the club. Others have praised the warm welcome and friendly environment.

As well as being a lively group in itself, JUICE has had an effect on the life of the church. Ongoing publicity is provided through two large display boards in the hall so that the congregation are kept in touch with the faces and the activities. Several young families came to the Christingle service, the number of baptisms is increasing and there are plans for a crèche. Colette looks forward to the day when the tiny 'Sunday school' is revitalized as the toddlers grow and become more involved in the life of the worshipping community.

6 No children in church

Are you sure?

If there are no children connected with your church the first question is to ask whether that is strictly true.

Contrary to popular opinion, children do come to church, but they are not always noticed or counted. Ask yourself if children are involved in any of these services at your church or use your church premises in association with any of the following:

- special services designed with children in mind, such as a Christingle or a Crib service, Mothering Sunday and Harvest Thanksgiving services;
- schools using the church for carol services and other services, or RE, history and English lessons;
- uniformed organizations coming to a Parade service on Remembrance Sunday and St George's Day;
- children coming to weddings, baptisms, and occasionally, funerals;
- parent and toddler or pre-school groups;
- uniformed organizations, drama, karate, and other groups meeting in the hall.

Growing from a small start

If the answer to any of these is 'Yes!', then you do have children coming to church or at least on your church premises. Start from where you are, not where you want to be. See that the welcome, helpfulness and the quality of worship they experience if they are at a service are of a level that makes them have good feelings about the church – and they may want to come again. Offer information about the church and its activities to the parents and group leaders.

Developing relationships

According to your situation, seek to develop your relationships with the groups of children and their leaders and families. This will vary according to the contacts you have at present. Take time and be patient. Your children's work of the past will have diminished over several years, maybe even decades. That sort of gradual neglect loses more than the children from the church. Children's leaders may have died or moved away and not been replaced, relationships with families and local schools will have declined. It will take planning, prayer and sheer hard work to start the ministry again.

Special services

If there are families coming to special services, consider offering them more often. If the number is small, check first whether there might be a better time that would attract more people. Visit the uniformed organizations before the Parade service to see how the youngsters can be involved in it through reading, choosing hymns or leading the prayers. When you have built up a rapport, invite them to take part in an event or come to another service.

It is unlikely that you will develop children's work from attendees at weddings or baptisms, but seek to give the children who come to them the same welcome and standard of worship as you give children on other occasions. Offer information about the next events and services. Some of the families will live in your parish and may return for a special service if they have felt welcomed and have good feelings about the service they have attended.

Schools

If the local school is using your church building for worship or lessons, you already have a relationship on which you can build. Have a couple of the congregation on hand to welcome and help. See that the building is warm. If the children come for a carol service, offer an Easter or a leavers' service. See whether the school can be more involved in the church, maybe by displaying artwork or providing music on Education Sunday or at another service. See whether the church can be of help in the school.

Groups and organizations

Seek to develop relationships with the groups that use your hall. The majority of leaders welcome links with the church. There will be, however, a few that do not for a variety of reasons and this must be respected. When you have built up a relationship, you will know the best way forward. It may be by offering a tiny service at the parent and toddler group or pre-school or inviting them to a Crib service on Christmas Eve. With uniformed organizations, the approach is similar. With groups that have less obvious entrées, it is a case of making it known that the church is available at times of need and inviting the groups to take part in church events, giving a dancing display or a karate demonstration for example.

Children at other churches

If you find that some of the children on the fringe of your church go to another church in the area, you may feel that this is the reason that you have no children. You may even feel envious! Do not assume that it has flourishing children's work and that everything is easy. No children's work just happens, and the youngsters there may be reaping the results of literally decades of steady work and prayer. Visit the church and ask the leaders about their children's ministry. Learn from their experience. See whether there is something that you can contribute, either by working together or by offering something that is different but needed in the community.

First steps

Having established relationships with the youngsters where you have some sort of contact, with the local school and other churches, move on by having a single event like a fun day. Take your time over this and forget any assumptions that Sunday is the best time and that the best place is church! If that were so, the children would probably be there already.

If you have school-aged children on your fringe, find out the times they are available and their needs. Consider whether a club with some Christian teaching as well as fun and games, held after school or on Saturday morning once a month, or a short family service in the early evening would be appropriate. Look at Chapter 8, 'Seven whole days', for ideas on various events and worship, and ways of planning them.

Give invitations to any children who have links with your church or use your hall. Ask if you can distribute them to the children at the local school. Advertise the event where children are to be found: the health centre, library, or, in a small village, by posting leaflets through every door where you know there are children.

Start at the bottom

In some communities where there is new property suitable for first-time buyers, you may find families with very young children but few of school age. On some housing estates, there are young mothers who feel trapped in high-rise blocks, maybe with their neighbours out all day. If that is the case, consider whether it would be better to start with a toddler club. Young mothers have often left work and friends to start their families and feel lonely and isolated so would appreciate the friendship that such a club would provide. Your local health visitor would advise you on whether such a club was needed.

Research and plan

Whatever you decide to do, research it carefully so that you are sure that you are reaching the children and their families where they are, in every sense. Turn to Chapter 8, 'Seven whole days', and Chapter 9, 'United we stand', to find ways of developing the suggestions in this chapter. There is a list of resources in Appendix B.

7 Communities with few children

No children in our hamlet

One of the saddest letters I received in my work as a children's adviser, came from a lady in a village in north Essex. I had written to all the Parochial Church Councils inviting representatives to attend a session on best practice in Child Protection. The letter, hand-written on blue writing paper, said courteously that this did not apply to her parish because there were not any children at the church … and then it added, 'or in our hamlet'. I sat quietly for a moment and then I turned to the diocesan directory. There were the parish statistics: population 65, electoral roll 10. It was literally a dying community.

That situation is, sadly, not unique and invokes sympathy for the faithful members of the community who have seen their village dwindle, amenities removed, and the young people move away to find work and affordable housing. The reasons behind this are far beyond the scope of this book but the situation brings home that children are seen as signs of life and hope for the future.

Childless communities

Communities with very few children fall into four basic groups. There are the inner city parishes, where there is little housing for families. These are often areas of deprivation and the residents are often largely of other faiths. At the other end of the scale are the very wealthy areas, where there is a high proportion of single professional people and the families that live there spend their weekends in the country.

In rural areas, there are the small villages like the one described above, where the population has shrunk and young people have moved away in search of work and better amenities for their families. In some other villages, however, much of the housing is taken up by the owners of second homes, who are not involved in daily village life and are unlikely to be attending the local church.

Urban areas

As many inner city churches are struggling for survival, children are only one item on a long list of challenges, but there are still ways of reaching the few youngsters that are in the community. It is foolish to attempt to provide a children's group on Sunday if there are not enough children living in the parish to make the work viable.

Church schools

Many inner city parishes and villages have Church schools. A good Church school will bring Christian light and hope to a deprived community. A strong relationship between the parish and its school can help to provide worship and teaching as well as witness through voluntary and paid help. This can involve more than the vicar taking assembly once a week. Members of the congregation can be governors, or employed as classroom assistants and midday meals supervisors, as well as providing voluntary help. As mentioned in the previous chapter, most of the links discussed here can apply to any school if a good relationship has been forged.

Encourage the staff to use the church for RE and other lessons, as well as services. If you have the resources, run a holiday club at the school. See that you keep families informed about the services at festivals and other church events. There is more information about this in Chapter 6, 'No children in church', and Chapter 8, 'Seven whole days'.

You may not directly increase your congregation through your relationship with your Church school in such an area, let alone develop a viable Junior Church, but you will have sent out a powerful Christian message to families that may need it. You may find that a few youngsters are attracted by the idea of serving or that the school can provide music or artwork for special occasions.

Nannies and au pairs

In some very wealthy urban areas, the children are usually cared for by nannies or au pairs. By the time that the children are about eight years old, either the family has moved out into the country or the children are at boarding school. The population in such an area is transient and the children's carers are the most stable part of the population, moving on from one local family to another as their charges grow up. This is an intensely lonely way of life, especially for au pairs who are far from home. A drop-in centre, toddler club or buggy service would provide a chance to chat with their fellow workers, as well as a place for the children to play together. It would also have a pastoral angle where lonely people could talk about problems knowing that they would find a sympathetic ear, assurance of confidentiality and practical advice.

Rural areas

In one sense the issue of tiny congregations in small communities has been addressed by parishes being put together in benefices, but that has often resulted in a lot of hurt and reluctance to work together, so combining forces to provide a viable children's group or Family Service each month may not be as straightforward as one might think. Cooperation is, however, the most realistic answer for that situation. Concentrate the children's ministry on the church that has most children and work across the benefice and even ecumenically.

The suggestions in the section on Church schools are applicable in rural as well as urban areas.

Mobile children's work

Some churches in rural areas run their children's work in a caravan or a bus that visits the different villages. Others have a car or minibus service that collects children and their families for a monthly service.

Many of the suggestions in Chapter 3, 'Sunday morning in church', and Chapter 8, 'Seven whole days', would become viable with cooperation between churches. The final chapter of this book, 'United we stand', explores this in detail.

Benefiting the children and the Church

The kinds of initiative described in this chapter involve imagination and cooperation. Some may demand courage and sacrifice as a community lets go of non-viable children's work, but this may well be best for the children and thereby for the future of the wider Church.

A story of courage: Letting go for the children's sake

The benefice of Toptree and Four Oaks with Aldridge consisted of three hamlets and a few farms. Each had a church but attendance was very small at all of them. One of the biggest concerns was that the number of children in each parish was too small for the church to cater for them properly. They met on special occasions, for a Christmas party and an Easter egg hunt, but the total number of youngsters in all the three churches was only eleven so separate groups were not sustainable on their own. Another factor was that some of the congregations still liked having services from the *Book of Common Prayer.*

The leaders decided that, because there was some new housing being built at Toptree, it would run a Junior Church and have a monthly Family Service in that church. If there were a viable group, it might attract some of the new families. Aldridge had a village hall so a benefice holiday club would be held there, followed by a special service in the summer holidays. Four Oaks would offer traditional worship. It would welcome children but make no special provision for them. A car rota was organized to take people to the church service of their choice.

This decision was costly, but it paved the way for a viable children's nurture group, as well as outreach among children in the community, and for everyone to attend the services that they preferred.

---

8 Seven whole days

Pressure on Sunday

We have already noted that there is heavy pressure on Sunday with flexible working, retail trading, sporting events, and mobile and widely spread families. An increasing number of children spend Sunday or the whole weekend with a second parent or even an entire second family. Parents whose partners do not attend church, have the added pressure of wanting to give time to their children and not letting church attendance become an issue in a crowded weekend. We have seen how the issue of very low and erratic attendance on Sundays can be resolved by having a monthly Family Service of some kind and a monthly Junior Church. This concentrates the children's work onto two Sundays each month and may well lead to higher attendance on those special occasions.

Is Sunday the best time?

A more radical approach is to consider whether, with all the pressures, Sunday morning is the best time for a Junior Church or similar activity. This is looking beyond the few children who already attend the church, towards those who for various reasons find it impractical to come to the church building on a Sunday morning. It moves beyond the worship and nurture into the church's mission among the children in the community.

Most of the alternatives would operate once a month rather than being a weekly event, but as they could run for a longer time, from an hour to a whole morning, there is still time for a meaningful level of Christian teaching and witness. A weekday or Saturday group will probably attract children who do not normally come to church so the style of teaching and whole atmosphere will be very different.

Saturday fun morning

Some churches have started having a monthly event on a Saturday morning with games and activities as well as Christian teaching. It lasts for about two hours, which allows parents to go shopping or do the usual weekly chores, while the children have a good time. Each event is free-standing, so there is less pressure on the children's leaders than providing a continuous programme for a group that fluctuates in attendance. More people are inclined to help if it is an occasional event and does not conflict with the Sunday service.

Midweek Junior Church

The whole pattern of after-school childcare is an enormous one. In this context, we are considering providing specific Christian nurture on a weekday after school. This would be especially appropriate if the community were a close-knit one where all the children attended the same primary school. The group could meet in a classroom or the school hall and have refreshments and games as well as Christian teaching. An alternative in an urban area would be for the group to be held at the church and the youngsters to be escorted from school by parents or helpers.

The whole subject of out-of-school care is an enormous one with government initiatives and funding. The Church can play a significant role in certain circumstances, but this is very different from the kind of activity described here. If a church wants to explore that subject, information can be found in *Not Just Sunday* (Church House Publishing, 2002).

Midweek worship

The aim of a Family Service is twofold: firstly to allow the whole Christian family regardless of age to worship together, and secondly to provide a more informal form of service that is accessible to people on the fringe of the church. Many are highly successful, but the chief disadvantage of them is that they are still held on Sunday morning in the church building.

Consider having a monthly service after school that is geared towards children and their parents. It could even be held on the school premises. It is an accessible building and a place and time when children and their younger siblings, parents and carers are together. Another possible time would be during an early evening. If you consider that option, find out the best time and day. It will depend on the social structure of your community;

whether a large number of people commute or work locally will be a main factor in deciding the time and structure.

Advantages of operating midweek

The advantage of these midweek groups is clear. They allow greater flexibility in the timing and style of the programme. They can respond to the needs and social life of the community and so almost certainly attract children on the fringe of the church and maybe some with no previous links. Holding the group less frequently than once a week should concentrate numbers and thereby make the group less fragile.

In some cases, it would be easier to get volunteer leaders and helpers, but that depends on whether they are in full-time work and on their other commitments.

Links with the church

The chief disadvantage of these groups is that they do not have such strong links with the main worshipping congregation. It is vital that the church council owns this work, and provides funding and support as it would for a group operating on a Sunday. Raise the profile by publishing the meetings or services in the church newsletter and including them in the prayers on the previous Sunday. Encourage as many people as possible to visit the group or help with it occasionally. The children in the group can pray for the rest of the church and display pictures or other work in the church building. They can also be given copies of the church newsletter and invitations to special services and events to take home.

If the group meets near to the church, one of the activities could be a 'treasure' hunt in the building. Many churches have stained-glass windows and memorial tablets. Nearly every church has an altar table, cross or crucifix, font, lectern, kneelers, robes and notice board. These could all be points for teaching about the way that Christians worship. If appropriate, prayer time could also be held in church on some occasions.

Connecting with the Sunday service

If a Saturday club were held on the day before the Family Service, it would be possible to provide links with the theme of the Sunday, or simply to invite the children to 'come tomorrow'.

For families who come occasionally, this might encourage them to set aside a special weekend each month. A few extra children might turn up, especially if they know what to expect or their work is going to be featured. Do not be disappointed, however, if they do not come. Build up a good rapport with them first, and be patient. Too much pressure can be counterproductive.

Occasional services

Lastly, consider holding an occasional Sunday afternoon service geared to the children and their families, for example Christingle, Mothering Sunday, Pentecost birthday service, or Harvest Thanksgiving, with refreshments afterwards.

Think differently

These suggestions are ways of reviewing your children's work and thinking differently about it. It is about alternatives rather than additions.

If the group on Sunday is fragile or hardly viable, consider whether it would be more successful on another day. The numbers may not be huge but twelve children meeting on a Friday afternoon, or a group of families worshipping on Wednesday after school, or twenty youngsters at a Saturday club are all ways of helping more children to hear the gospel story. A quarterly service on a Sunday afternoon with tea afterwards may suit your congregation better than a monthly Family Service that is not well attended.

It is always difficult to challenge patterns that have been held for generations, even though the world has moved on. None of these ideas is financially costly but they all involve change. That takes courage and planning.

9 United we stand

Working together

So far, we have discussed how a church can celebrate and value its small group of children, and ways in which it could strengthen its ministry by concentrating on a couple of Sundays each month, or by holding the Junior Church on another day and maybe in another place. We have also reviewed the Church's role in communities with very few children. In all of these cases, a solution is for two or more churches to explore ways of working together or even providing a joint children's ministry.

It is a sad fact that Christians are not very good at working with other people. This includes their fellow Christians in other churches. However, with more churches being clustered into benefices, team ministries and local ecumenical groups, the structure is already in place, even if it is not maximized.

In areas with several churches where the children's ministry is struggling, or in rural and inner city areas where there are very few children, the best answer will be for the local churches to work together. This not always easy and any steps have to be taken carefully. Joint activities are often seen as a confession of failure and an undermining of something precious that is part of the local heritage. Sensitivity and affirmation of present and past ministries is vital if any move towards cooperation beyond an occasional event is to be supported by the congregation as a whole.

Start by questioning whether your small group of youngsters is unsustainable or whether it is just not obviously effective. Then review the children's work in the whole area, and talk to your ecumenical colleagues or the other churches in your deanery. Consider whether there are ways of working as a benefice or a deanery or ecumenically.

It is OK to be a Christian

Apart from the obvious benefit of sharing resources and bringing the children together, there are hidden benefits. Children who go to church are a minority. A youngster may be the only one in his or her class that attends any place of worship, and it is certainly not something that is considered trendy or 'cool' by peers. Bringing Christian children together for any reason helps youngsters to see that they are not odd or different from other children: there are others like them, maybe living in the same street or attending the same school. Children's leaders can feel very isolated and many have low self-esteem. Bringing them together boosts morale and can offer them a source of support and advice.

As every situation is different, rather than providing detailed advice, here are a few suggestions that could act as springboards to discussion and planning:

Playing together

Organize an outing for the children of the local churches. This could be as simple as a tea party or a picnic with games, or could be a visit to a place of interest or a pantomime. If two churches work closely together, for example through being in the same village, and have enough children of similar age, it could be worth having a sleepover on a Saturday night with the children going to their own churches or for a joint service on the next morning.

Whatever you plan, see that you have enough adults to look after the children or help with activities. If your outing includes games or sports, do not have children over eleven years playing with children under seven years, for safety reasons.

Have a fun morning for all the local churches or the benefice. Hold it in the church hall with the best facilities or in a school. If the area is far-flung, it may be necessary to organize a car run or even a minibus to transport the children.

The level of Christian teaching will be your decision, but it is important for the children to realize the importance of enjoying each other's company and playing together. Have games and activities for the different age groups and include refreshments. Take photographs that can be displayed in each church and send them to the local newspaper. If the theme of the morning is biblical, the children could take songs or artwork back to their own churches on the next Sunday.

Festivals and pilgrimages

If your diocese has a children's festival, take the children. Children's advisers are always delighted when churches with just a few children sign up for these events and welcome even a single family from a parish. Encourage other churches to come with you so that you travel as a group.

Places of pilgrimage such as Walsingham, Iona and other local shrines hold events geared towards young people. Meeting literally hundreds of other young Christians in a special place is a rewarding and emotional experience that will encourage children and adults alike. The feedback from a festival or pilgrimage would supply nurture sessions and Family Services for some weeks.

Local events

If several events have been successful, consider whether the churches of a whole district or deanery could combine forces to hold a local festival. This would provide a tailor-made way for the children to enjoy activities that they could not do in their own churches. It could be planned like a fun morning, but include some special activities such as a bouncy castle or sports. It could last all day and groups and families could bring a picnic lunch. It encourages the local churches to build on the fact that there are more Christian children in the locality than the children had realized. It also gives a feeling of achievement to the children's workers who have organized it.

Be warned, however, that festivals need careful, long-term preparation. Book the date and venue at least nine months in advance and allow six months for preparation. Ask your children's adviser or people who have organized this sort of event before to help you. It will be hard work, but the rewards will be great.

Ongoing cooperation

Children's leaders in a district or deanery could meet termly to plan work, share ideas or just to have a meal. This could include training on the particular needs of small churches.

Small churches tend to be under-resourced. Help can be given by sharing books and lending equipment or by having an email group.

'Lend a leader' has been used between churches where one is either starting some children's work or is struggling to maintain it. A leader from a larger church comes to help with the children's ministry, by working alongside the present leader, providing hands-on training and offering expertise and experience for any time between three and six months. Arranging this will depend on your particular situation and needs but your diocesan or denominational children's adviser would provide advice if you needed guidance.

In a benefice of several churches, consider concentrating the children's ministry to one church, with a Junior Church and Family Service held there each month. It would be sensible if that were where most of the youngsters were living or where there were the best facilities. This does not mean that the other churches have nothing. They may have links with a school, run a holiday club or offer an occasional special service, but the weekly provision will be elsewhere.

Ecumenical children's work

Similarly, work ecumenically in a community where there are two churches close together. An ecumenical Junior Church could be held in the village hall, community centre or the church with better facilities. This could take place on Sunday morning or, as already suggested, as a Saturday club. Children could still go on to their own church's service afterwards or the churches could take turns to hold a Family Service.

Combined operations

A general guideline is to cooperate rather than compete. Helping with another church's toddler group or leading the local Beaver colony may be effective evangelism and is certainly better witness than setting up another activity in competition. In addition, one small but strong group is more likely to flourish than two weak ones.

If you can see a need but have not the numbers of children or resources to sustain meeting it, talk to another church and see if you can work together. As well as the single events, consider having a holiday club, Saturday morning activity days, or providing a club linked with the local school.

Cooperation for the greater good

The difficulty in cooperating or letting go, comes when considering children's work on Sunday, the Sunday school or Junior Church. We are so wedded to the idea of the children being there in the hall on Sunday morning, that we forget that this has only been common for the last fifteen years and that most traditional Sunday schools before then had few links with the worshipping congregation. Children are seen, quite correctly, as signs of hope for the future. However, the Church is bigger than the individual church building. If it is in the children's interests to combine with another church or even let the youngsters go, that future is more positive than clinging on to a small disaffected group.

This kind of step takes courage and it means sacrifice, but our intention is to do the Lord's work in proclaiming the Good News to our young people, and that has no boundaries or traditions.

> 'there is hope for your future, says the Lord: your children shall come back to their own country.'
>
> *Jeremiah 31.17*

A story of witness: Rosie's club

Rosie was the school-crossing lady. She was a good listener with an outgoing personality so parents often stopped to have a chat with her. In fact, they often told her their problems and about the strains of bringing up young families in high-rise flats with all the pressures of a fast-moving and demanding world. Rosie began to realize that, in her conversations, she was sharing her faith with the young parents and their children. She also realized that many of the parents were stressed because there was nowhere for their children to play safely on their own.

There were rarely any children at Rosie's church. She knew that she would not be able to persuade the children to come on Sunday, and, any rate, that was not where the need was. She asked the vicar if she could use the hall for an hour on every Friday afternoon, and so the ASK (After School Kids) club was born.

Eight years later, the club is operating three times a week and running a two-week play scheme in the summer holidays. It has a staff of six and nearly forty children. It has a strong Christian ethos and the children themselves provide service to the wider community. This ranges from helping to turn the wasteland behind the hall into a garden to making a mile of pennies for the local children's hospice. The church actively supports the work and it receives grants from the local authority and a children's charity.

Rosie is now in her mid-seventies and has retired from hands-on work, but has kept an interest in the club. She has the satisfaction of seeing how her Christian witness to a small group of needy families in the community has developed into a thriving ministry among children in which the church is serving the whole parish.

The golden rules

Very few methods of engaging with children are completely right or wrong. Each church is different and what is a success in one situation may be ineffective in another. There are, however, a few golden rules that need to be kept in mind if your children's work is to be viable and develop.

1. Value each child as an individual and a blessing. Welcome every contact that your church has with children. Accept their ministry and you will receive all you have given and much more.

2. Always be positive. It is not a case of having 'only three children', but that three is more than one or two, and a lot more than having nobody.

3. Be prepared to change. A children's ministry does not just happen. A church with children is very different from one without them and such a change will affect everyone.

4. Never say that something is not worth doing for such a small number. It negates Jesus' teaching about the value of the sparrow, the widow's mite and, indeed, the child. On a pragmatic level, while you wait for large numbers before taking action, you will wait forever!

5. If the youngsters are welcomed and valued as part of the church family, they will have positive feelings about being a Christian that will last for all of their lives.

6. When you are disappointed by small numbers, do not show that you feel disheartened. Saying, 'Good, we can all get around one table', or 'We have so many Easter eggs that you can each have two' makes the children feel special. Listing the people who are missing makes those present feel undervalued and almost guarantees that they will lose interest.

7. A ministry among children is one of the most difficult and creative in the Church. In other words, it is hard work. It is also one of the most rewarding as a child grows in faith and love of God.

8.   Think of the wise bridesmaids and be prepared. If new children appear at your church, and there is nothing for them, they will go elsewhere. Next week is too late!

Remembering and acting upon those golden rules may seem almost impossible when numbers and facilities are small. They are, however, the guidelines for anything to succeed, whether in church or in commerce.

Having faith

Maybe your church is making tremendous efforts but somehow they do not seem to succeed. Do not feel that you have failed. Mission is long-term work and the Holy Spirit works in its own way and at its own time.

If each one of your youngsters, however few there are, has been welcomed as a member of your worshipping community and given an experience of the presence of God, this is something that they will never lose. They may stay with you or they may disappear, only to return at a later date, or in another place. They may be the means of more children hearing the Christian story in a few years' time, or pass it on to the next generation in another place.

> Give ear, O my people, to my teaching; incline your ears to the words of my mouth. I will open my mouth in a parable; I will utter dark sayings from of old, things that we have heard and known, that our ancestors have told us. We will not hide them from their children; we will tell to the coming generation the glorious deeds of the Lord, and his might, and the wonders that he has done. He established a decree in Jacob, and appointed a law in Israel, which he commanded our ancestors to teach to their children; that the next generation might know them, the children yet unborn, and rise up and tell them to their children, so that they should set their hope in God, and not forget the works of God, but keep his commandments …
>
> *Psalm 78.1-7*

Further resources

There are very few organizations and resources to support a ministry among a small number of children and the needs of small churches. However, the following organizations and books will be of help.

Organizations
Children's work advisers

Every Anglican diocese and major denomination has a designated person to advise on children's work. Most are employed either full- or part-time; a few are volunteers. They will advise on all matters, including resources, provide consultancy to individual parishes, training courses for leaders, and events for children. A few dioceses have resources for loan or purchase.

Consult your Diocesan or Denominational Handbook or web site for further information.

CURBS

CURBS (Children in URBan Situations) produces Christian resources, including activity packs, known as CURBStone Kits, geared to the needs of children in inner cities and urban estates. It also provides advice, networking and a vision for children's work, set in the context of ongoing support and training of leaders.

4 Hawksmoor Close, London, E6 5SL

Tel: 07941 336589

Email: info@.curbsproject.org.uk

Web site: www.curbsproject.org.uk

Godly Play

Godly Play originated in the USA through the work of Jerome Berryman and now has several centres and tutors in the UK. It offers one-day and three-day courses, advice and resources.

Contact through the web site: www.godlyplay.org.uk

Rural Sunrise

This is part of Rural Ministries, an ecumenical organization, which specializes in small and rural churches. It advises on strategic planning, fun days, holiday and midweek clubs, as well as leading children's events. It also produces biblically based resources.

2 The Old Forge, Gardner Street, Hailsham, East Sussex, BN27 4LE

Tel: 01323 832445

Email: barry@ruralmissions.org.uk

Web site: www.ruralmissions.org.uk

Scripture Union

A major non-denominational evangelistic organization that provides advice, training, hands-on work, and resources. Its publications include a large number for use with children.

207–209 Queensway, Bletchley, Milton Keynes, MK2 2EB

Tel: 01908 856000

Email: info@scriptureunion.org.uk

Web site: www.scriptureunion.org.uk

Useful publications
Handbooks on children's ministry
Simon Bass, *Special Children, Special Needs: Integrating children with disabilities and special needs into your church*, Church House Publishing, 2003.

Francis Bridger, *Children Finding Faith*, Scripture Union, 2000.

Kathryn Copsey, *Become Like a Child*, Scripture Union, 1994.

Wendy Duffy, *Children and Bereavement*, Church House Publishing, 2003.

Mike Law, *Small Groups Growing Churches*, Scripture Union, 2003.

Margaret Withers, *Where Are the Children?*, BRF, forthcoming 2005.

Gretchen Wolff Pritchard, *Offering the Gospel to Children*, Cowley, 1992.

Leadership training
Margaret Withers, *Fired Up not burnt out*, BRF, 2001.

Midweek ministry
Margaret Withers, *Not Just Sunday: Setting up and running mid-week clubs for children*, Church House Publishing, 2002.

Gillian Wood, *Linking Churches and Schools*, Churches Together in England, 2003.

Nurture materials suitable for small groups
Jerome W. Berryman, *Teaching Godly Play*, Abingdon, 1995.

David Bolster, *A Fresh Encounter,* Scripture Union, 2003.

Gillian Chapman, *Celebrations Make and Do*, BRF, 2004.

Lance Pierson, *Growing Through Change*, Scripture Union, 2003.

Programmes suitable for all ages
Light for a New Generation

Scripture Union, 2004. For more information see the web site,
www.scriptureunion.org.uk

Roots

Ecumenically created programme distributed by bimonthly
for Churches Ltd.
For more information see the web site, www.rootsontheweb.com
Single copies available from bookshops or subscriptions from *Roots*
subscriptions, 4 John Wesley Road, Peterborough, PE4 6ZP

Tel: 01733 325002

email: sales@rootsontheweb.com

Worship

The Communion Cube, Church House Publishing, 2003.

The Lord's Prayer Cube, Church House Publishing, 2004.

Anne Faulkner, *My Book of Special Times in Church*, BRF, 1999.

Diana Murrie, *My Communion Book*, Church House Publishing, 2002.

Betty Pedley and John Muir, *Children in the Church?*, Church House
Publishing, 1997.

Neil Pugmire and Mark Rodel, *Launchpad*, BRF, 2004.

Margaret Withers, *Welcome to the Lord's Table*, BRF, 1999.

Index

Other resources for children's work

Each book in this series provides a short, practical introduction to a key aspect of the Church's work with children and includes sources of further help and information for those who want to take the subject further.

Not Just Sunday

Setting up and running
mid-week clubs for children
Margaret Withers
£3.95   0 7151 4982 2
This book gives basic information about setting up and organizing mid-week clubs for children. As well as offering guidance on the first steps of planning and running mid-week children's activities, it gives advice about legal matters, funding and training.

Special Children, Special Needs

Integrating children with disabilities
and special needs into your church
Simon Bass
£5.95   0 7151 4999 7
Simon Bass uses his extensive experience to provide essential information on how to integrate children with special needs into your church and its children's programmes and activities.

Children and Bereavement

(2nd edition)
Wendy Duffy
£6.95   0 7151 4998 9
This sensitive guide examines the needs of bereaved children of different ages, their reactions to death and the stages of their grief. This second edition includes completely new sections on dealing with tragic events such as September 11 and Soham.

Protecting All God's Children

(3rd edition)
The Child Protection Policy
for the Church of England
House of Bishops
£5.95   0 7151 3867 7
The third edition of the House of Bishops' Policy on Child Protection is intended to ensure that all children who have contact with the Church of England are safeguarded. It contains the revised House of Bishops' Policy on Child Protection, together with a series of procedures for dioceses and parishes to follow.

For more information visit the Children and Young People Section at www.chpublishing.co.uk